My Pet Baby Turtles

How to Handle Pet Baby Turtles

by

Anish Dhiran Muhunthan,

Ashthan Harry Muhunthan,

and Shamgi Muhunthan

DORRANCE
PUBLISHING CO
EST. 1920
PITTSBURGH, PENNSYLVANIA 15238

Dorrance Publishing Co
585 Alpha Drive
Pittsburgh, PA 15238
Visit our website at www.dorrancebookstore.com

ISBN: 978-1-6366-1526-4
eISBN: 978-1-6366-1701-5

My Pet Baby Turtles

How to Handle Pet Baby Turtles

My brother's name is Ashthan Harry. He is six years old. We have a pet at home. Our pet dog's name is Snowy. It's a female dog known as a Maltese. I'd like to have another pet. It's a sea turtle.

In general, a female turtle lays her eggs in the land close to the beach. The female sea turtle covers them up with sand then leaves them. After laying the eggs, the mother turtle's work is done. The baby turtles must survive by themselves.

It takes around two months for eggs to hatch.

A baby sea turtle is known as a hatchling.

Sea turtle hatchlings eat a variety of food like seaweeds, jellyfish, and fish eggs. If I had a sea turtle, I would feed my turtle daily. I'd put their food in the water. I'd offer a variety of food to hatchlings like carrots, cucumber, beef, and shrimp, all cut in small pieces. I researched this information on the internet.

You can tell a sea turtle is male or female by looking at the tail. Male sea turtles have long thick tails and long nails on their front feet. Female sea turtles have short thin tails and very short nails.

Be aware baby sea turtles can drown in the water. They can hold their breath for a very long time, but they have to come up to breathe, otherwise they will drown.

Do not put sea turtles in cold water; they will get sick. You can make a large aquarium with shallow water for a swimming area.

A sea turtle can hear too. A sea turtle does not need a friend to be happy. The sea turtle is an endangered species. It's illegal to harm or kill a sea turtle.

SAVE SEA TURTLES!
DO NOT POLLUTE THE WATER AND LAND.

If I had a sea turtle, I would love my sea turtle every day. I would name her Gemba. I'd like to have another male sea turtle, a boy whose name would be Jayran.

The End!